THEORY
OF SUPPLY

Wealth Mastery: 20 Paths to Financial Freedom

Table of Contents

Introduction

Creating and sticking to a budget for effective money management.

Understanding the power of compound interest and long-term investing.

Diversifying investments to minimize risk and maximize returns.

Developing a mindset of abundance and wealth consciousness.

Leveraging tax-efficient strategies to optimize wealth growth.

Building multiple streams of passive income for financial security.

Utilizing debt wisely to leverage investments and assets.

Investing in assets with intrinsic value, such as real estate and precious metals.

Harnessing the potential of entrepreneurship for wealth creation.

Implementing strategies for wealth preservation and intergenerational wealth transfer.

Cultivating financial discipline and resilience in the face of market volatility.

Incorporating philanthropy and giving into your wealth mastery journey.

Navigating the psychology of money: understanding emotions and biases.

Mastering negotiation skills for maximizing income and investment opportunities.

Developing a personalized investment strategy aligned with your risk tolerance and financial goals.

Embracing continuous learning and staying updated on financial trends and opportunities.

Creating a legacy plan to leave behind a lasting impact on future generations.

Practicing mindfulness and gratitude in managing wealth and abundance.

Building a supportive network of mentors and peers for ongoing education and accountability.

Introduction:

"Wealth Mastery: Navigating 20 Paths to Financial Freedom" is a comprehensive guidebook that empowers readers to take control of their financial destiny and embark on a journey towards wealth and abundance. Drawing on insights from personal finance experts, wealth advisors, and thought leaders, this book offers practical strategies, actionable advice, and inspirational stories to help readers achieve financial independence, build lasting wealth, and leave a legacy that transcends generations.

From setting SMART financial goals to mastering negotiation skills, diversifying investments, and cultivating a mindset of abundance, each chapter explores key principles and practices for navigating the complexities of wealth management and personal finance. Readers will learn how to develop a personalized investment strategy aligned with their goals and risk tolerance, harness the power of compound interest and long-term investing, and leverage tax-efficient strategies to optimize wealth growth.

In addition to practical financial guidance, "Wealth Mastery" emphasizes the importance of mindfulness, gratitude, and continuous learning in managing wealth and abundance. Readers will discover how practicing mindfulness and gratitude can enhance their financial well-being, foster a sense of abundance consciousness, and cultivate meaningful relationships with mentors and peers for ongoing education and accountability.

Whether you're a seasoned investor or just starting on your financial journey, "Wealth Mastery" provides the tools, insights, and inspiration you need to navigate the complexities of wealth management, overcome obstacles, and achieve true financial freedom. With a holistic approach to wealth mastery that integrates financial expertise with personal development principles, this book empowers readers to unlock their full potential, create a life of abundance, and leave a lasting legacy for future generations.

1. Setting SMART Financial Goals for Wealth Accumulation

Financial success doesn't happen by chance. It's the result of careful planning, disciplined execution, and setting clear, actionable goals. Whether you're aiming to retire comfortably, buy a home, start a business, or achieve any other financial milestone, setting SMART goals can significantly increase your chances of success.

SMART is an acronym that stands for Specific, Measurable, Achievable, Relevant, and Time-bound. When applied to financial goals, it provides a structured framework that guides your efforts and keeps you on track. Let's delve deeper into each component of SMART financial goal setting:

Specific:

The first step in setting a SMART financial goal is to make it specific. Vague goals like "I want to be rich" or "I want to save more money" lack clarity and direction. Instead, define exactly what you want to achieve. For example, "I want to accumulate $1 million in retirement savings by age 60" is a specific goal that provides a clear target to aim for.

Measurable:

A goal must be measurable to track your progress and determine whether you're on course to achieve it. Measurable goals are quantifiable, allowing you to gauge your success over time. Using the previous example, you can measure your progress by tracking your retirement savings balance regularly and comparing it to your target of $1 million.

Achievable:

While it's important to set ambitious goals, they must also be achievable within your means. Assess your current financial situation, income, expenses, and resources to ensure that your goal is realistic. Setting an unattainable goal can lead to frustration and disappointment. Consider factors such as your earning potential, investment returns, and time horizon when determining achievability.

Relevant:

A relevant goal is one that aligns with your values, priorities, and long-term objectives. It should be meaningful and contribute to your overall financial well-being. For instance, if your priority is to become debt-free, setting a goal to pay off high-interest credit card debt would be more relevant than investing in speculative ventures. Ensure that your financial goals reflect your personal aspirations and financial circumstances.

Time-bound:

Lastly, every financial goal should have a specific timeframe for completion. Without a deadline, there's no sense of urgency, and procrastination can derail your progress. Establishing a timeframe creates accountability and motivates you to take consistent action towards your goal. Whether it's months, years, or decades, set a realistic deadline that provides a sense of challenge without overwhelming you.

Putting SMART Goals into Practice:

Now that we understand the components of SMART financial goals, let's apply them to a real-life scenario:

Example: Saving for a Down Payment on a Home

Specific: Instead of saying "I want to buy a house," specify the type of house you want and the amount of down payment required. For instance, "I want to save $50,000 for a 20% down payment on a three-bedroom house in my desired neighborhood."

Measurable: Break down your goal into smaller milestones, such as saving $10,000 per year for the next five years. Track your progress regularly by monitoring your savings account balance and adjusting your budget as needed.

Achievable: Evaluate your current financial situation to determine if saving $10,000 per year is feasible. If not, consider adjusting your timeline or exploring ways to increase your income or reduce expenses to make the goal more attainable.

Relevant: Assess whether homeownership aligns with your long-term goals and priorities. Consider factors such as stability, investment potential, and lifestyle preferences to ensure that buying a home is a relevant goal for you.

Time-bound: Set a deadline for achieving your goal, such as five years from now. Having a specific timeframe will help you stay focused and disciplined in your savings efforts.

Tips for Success:

Write Down Your Goals: Documenting your financial goals increases accountability and serves as a constant reminder of what you're working towards.

Break Down Complex Goals: If your goal seems overwhelming, break it down into smaller, more manageable tasks to avoid feeling discouraged.

Review and Adjust Regularly: Life circumstances and priorities change over time, so it's essential to review your goals periodically and make adjustments as needed.

Celebrate Milestones: Celebrating small victories along the way can boost morale and keep you motivated to continue pursuing your goals.

In conclusion, setting SMART financial goals lays the foundation for wealth accumulation and financial freedom. By making your goals Specific, Measurable, Achievable, Relevant, and Time-bound, you empower yourself to take control of your finances and turn your dreams into reality. Remember, the journey to financial success is a marathon, not a sprint, so stay disciplined, stay focused, and stay committed to achieving your goals.

2. Creating and Sticking to a Budget: The Key to Effective Money Management

Budgeting is the cornerstone of financial stability and success. It's a proactive approach to managing your money that allows you to allocate resources wisely, track your spending, and achieve your financial goals. However, creating a budget is just the first step; sticking to it requires discipline, consistency, and a willingness to make informed choices. In this article, we'll explore the importance of budgeting and provide practical tips for creating and adhering to a budget for effective money management.

The Importance of Budgeting:

A budget serves as a roadmap for your financial journey, guiding you towards your desired destination. Here are some key reasons why budgeting is crucial:

Financial Awareness: A budget provides clarity on where your money is going, allowing you to identify areas where you can save or cut back on expenses.

Goal Setting: By allocating funds towards specific financial goals, such as saving for a down payment on a house or paying off debt, a budget helps you stay focused and motivated.

Emergency Preparedness: Having a budget enables you to build an emergency fund, providing a safety net for unexpected expenses or financial setbacks.

Debt Management: A budget can help you prioritize debt repayment by allocating extra funds towards high-interest debt, accelerating your journey towards financial freedom.

Steps to Creating a Budget:

Assess Your Income: Start by calculating your total monthly income, including salaries, bonuses, side hustles, and any other sources of revenue.

List Your Expenses: Next, identify all your monthly expenses, including fixed costs like rent/mortgage, utilities, insurance, and variable expenses such as groceries, dining out, entertainment, and transportation.

Differentiate Needs vs. Wants: Distinguish between essential expenses (needs) and discretionary spending (wants). While needs are non-negotiable, wants can be adjusted to align with your financial goals.

Set Financial Goals: Determine your short-term and long-term financial objectives, such as saving for retirement, buying a car, or taking a vacation. Allocate funds towards each goal based on priority and feasibility.

Track Your Spending: Keep track of your expenses by recording every purchase, either manually or using budgeting apps or software. Review your spending regularly to identify areas where you can cut back or make adjustments.

Adjust as Needed: Be flexible with your budget and willing to make changes as circumstances change. Life is unpredictable, and your budget should reflect your evolving needs and priorities.

Tips for Sticking to Your Budget:

Be Realistic: Set realistic spending limits that reflect your income and financial obligations. Unrealistic expectations can lead to frustration and abandonment of your budgeting efforts.

Prioritize Your Goals: Focus on your most important financial goals and allocate resources accordingly. It's okay to say no to non-essential expenses if they detract from your long-term objectives.

Automate Savings: Set up automatic transfers from your checking account to your savings or investment accounts to ensure consistent savings each month.

Use Cash Envelopes: Allocate cash for discretionary spending categories like groceries, dining out, and entertainment. Once the cash envelope is empty, refrain from spending in that category until the next budget cycle.

Practice Delayed Gratification: Before making a purchase, ask yourself if it aligns with your budget and financial goals. If it's not a necessity, consider delaying the purchase or finding a more affordable alternative.

Stay Accountable: Share your budgeting goals with a trusted friend, family member, or financial advisor who can provide support and accountability.

Overcoming Challenges:

Sticking to a budget isn't always easy, and you may encounter obstacles along the way. Here are some common challenges and strategies for overcoming them:

Unexpected Expenses: Build an emergency fund to cover unforeseen costs and avoid derailing your budget.

Impulse Spending: Practice mindfulness and self-discipline to resist impulse purchases and stay focused on your financial goals.

Social Pressure: Be honest with friends and family about your budgeting goals and prioritize experiences that align with your budget.

Income Fluctuations: Plan for irregular income by budgeting based on your average monthly earnings and adjusting as necessary during lean months.

Final Thoughts:

Creating and sticking to a budget requires dedication, discipline, and a willingness to prioritize your financial well-being. By taking control of your money and aligning your spending with your values and goals, you can achieve financial freedom and peace of mind. Remember that budgeting is not about deprivation; it's about making intentional choices that empower you to live the life you desire while building a secure financial future. Start today by creating a budget that works for you, and commit to sticking to it for a brighter financial tomorrow.

3. Harnessing the Power of Compound Interest and Long-Term Investing

Compound interest is often hailed as the "eighth wonder of the world" by renowned physicist Albert Einstein, and for good reason. It's a phenomenon that can turn small investments into substantial wealth over time. When combined with a long-term investment strategy, compound interest has the potential to yield significant returns and pave the way for financial independence. In this article, we'll explore the concept of compound interest, its impact on investment growth, and the benefits of long-term investing.

Understanding Compound Interest:

Compound interest is the process whereby the interest on an investment or loan is calculated based on both the initial principal and the accumulated interest from previous periods. In other words, you earn interest not only on your original investment but also on the interest it generates over time. This compounding effect accelerates the growth of your investment exponentially, especially when allowed to accumulate over long periods.

The Power of Time in Investing:

Time is a crucial factor when it comes to harnessing the full potential of compound interest. The longer your money remains invested, the greater the impact of compounding. Consider the following example to illustrate this point:

Let's say you invest $10,000 in a diversified portfolio with an average annual return of 8%. After 10 years, your investment would grow to approximately $21,589. However, if you leave the money invested for 20 years, it would balloon to around $46,610. And if you have the patience to keep it invested for 30 years, it could soar to an impressive $100,627. This demonstrates how time can magnify the effects of compound interest and significantly increase your investment returns.

Benefits of Long-Term Investing:

Maximizing Compound Growth: Long-term investing allows you to fully capitalize on the power of compound interest. By giving your investments time to grow and compound, you can achieve exponential wealth accumulation over the years.

Reducing Market Volatility: Investing for the long term enables you to ride out short-term market fluctuations and volatility. Over extended periods, the impact of market downturns tends to be mitigated by periods of growth, resulting in smoother, more consistent returns.

Minimizing Transaction Costs: Frequent buying and selling of investments incur transaction costs such as brokerage fees and taxes, which can eat into your returns. Long-term investors typically have lower turnover in their portfolios, reducing transaction costs and maximizing net gains.

Benefiting from Dollar-Cost Averaging: Investing regularly over time, regardless of market conditions, allows you to take advantage of dollar-cost averaging. This strategy involves buying more shares when prices are low and fewer shares when prices are high, resulting in a lower average cost per share over time.

Building Wealth for Retirement: Long-term investing is especially crucial for retirement planning. By starting early and consistently contributing to retirement accounts such as 401(k)s and IRAs, you can build a substantial nest egg to support your lifestyle in retirement.

Strategies for Long-Term Investing:

Start Early: The earlier you begin investing, the more time your money has to grow. Even small contributions made early on can have a significant impact on your long-term wealth accumulation.

Stay Invested: Resist the temptation to react impulsively to short-term market fluctuations. Stick to your investment plan and maintain a long-term perspective, focusing on your financial goals rather than short-term noise.

Diversify Your Portfolio: Spread your investments across a variety of asset classes, such as stocks, bonds, real estate, and alternative investments. Diversification helps reduce risk and enhance long-term returns.

Reinvest Dividends and Capital Gains: Instead of cashing out dividends and capital gains, reinvest them back into your portfolio to take advantage of compounding. This allows your investment to grow more rapidly over time.

Review and Rebalance Regularly: Periodically review your investment portfolio to ensure it remains aligned with your risk tolerance and financial goals. Rebalance as needed to maintain diversification and optimize performance.

Conclusion:

Compound interest and long-term investing are powerful wealth-building strategies that can transform your financial future. By understanding the principles of compounding and committing to a disciplined, long-term investment approach, you can harness the full potential of your money and achieve your financial goals. Remember, investing is a journey, not a destination, so stay patient, stay focused, and let time and compounding work their magic to secure your financial success.

4. Diversifying Investments: Mitigating Risk and Enhancing Returns

Investing is inherently associated with risk. However, savvy investors understand that risk can be managed and minimized through diversification. Diversifying investments involves spreading your money across different asset classes, sectors, and geographic regions to reduce exposure to any single investment or market downturn. By diversifying effectively, investors can achieve a balance between risk and return, ultimately maximizing their long-term investment outcomes. In this article, we'll delve into the importance of diversification, its benefits, and strategies for implementing a diversified investment portfolio.

Understanding Diversification:

Diversification is the practice of investing in a variety of assets with different risk and return characteristics. The goal is to create a portfolio that is not overly reliant on any single investment or asset class, thereby reducing the overall risk of loss. While diversification cannot eliminate risk entirely, it can help mitigate the impact of adverse market events and improve the consistency of investment returns over time.

Benefits of Diversification:

Risk Reduction: Diversification spreads risk across multiple investments, reducing the potential impact of a decline in any single asset or sector. By avoiding overconcentration in one area, investors can safeguard their portfolios against significant losses.

Enhanced Returns: Diversification can improve risk-adjusted returns by combining assets with different return patterns. While some investments may experience downturns, others may perform well, offsetting losses and smoothing out overall portfolio returns.

Stability and Consistency: A diversified portfolio tends to be more stable and consistent over time, as it is less susceptible to the volatility of individual securities or sectors. This stability can provide investors with peace of mind and confidence in their long-term investment strategy.

Adaptability to Changing Market Conditions: Different assets may perform differently under various market conditions. By diversifying across asset classes and geographic regions, investors can adapt to changing market environments and capitalize on opportunities for growth while mitigating downside risk.

Strategies for Diversifying Investments:

Asset Allocation: Allocate your investments across different asset classes, such as stocks, bonds, real estate, and cash equivalents. Each asset class has unique risk and return characteristics, allowing you to achieve a balance between growth and stability in your portfolio.

Sector Diversification: Within each asset class, diversify across sectors and industries to minimize exposure to sector-specific risks. For example, instead of investing solely in technology stocks, consider allocating funds to sectors like healthcare, consumer staples, and industrials.

Geographic Diversification: Invest in assets from different geographic regions to reduce country-specific risks and benefit from global economic growth. International stocks and emerging market investments can provide diversification benefits and exposure to new markets and industries.

Individual Security Selection: Avoid overconcentration in individual stocks or securities by spreading your investments across a broad range of companies or issuers. Consider factors such as market capitalization, industry exposure, and company fundamentals when selecting individual securities for your portfolio.

Use of Investment Vehicles: Utilize investment vehicles such as mutual funds, exchange-traded funds (ETFs), and index funds to gain exposure to diversified portfolios of assets. These investment vehicles offer instant diversification and professional management at a low cost, making them suitable for both novice and experienced investors.

Rebalancing: Regularly review and rebalance your investment portfolio to maintain your desired asset allocation and risk profile. Rebalancing involves selling assets that have become overweight and reinvesting the proceeds into underweight assets to realign your portfolio with your investment objectives.

Conclusion:

Diversification is a fundamental principle of prudent investing that can help investors manage risk and enhance returns over the long term. By spreading investments across different asset classes, sectors, and geographic regions, investors can reduce exposure to specific risks and improve the consistency of investment returns. While diversification cannot guarantee profits or eliminate losses, it is an essential tool for building resilient and sustainable investment portfolios. Whether you're a novice investor or a seasoned professional, incorporating diversification into your investment strategy can help you achieve your financial goals while minimizing the impact of market volatility. Remember, the key to successful diversification is patience, discipline, and a long-term perspective.

5. Cultivating Abundance: Nurturing a Wealth Consciousness

In a world often characterized by scarcity and competition, cultivating a mindset of abundance and wealth consciousness can be transformative. Rather than viewing wealth as a finite resource, individuals with an abundance mindset recognize the boundless opportunities for growth, prosperity, and fulfillment that surround them. By embracing abundance, individuals can unlock their full potential, attract abundance into their lives, and achieve greater levels of success and happiness. In this article, we'll explore the concept of abundance mindset, its benefits, and practical strategies for developing wealth consciousness.

Understanding Abundance Mindset:

An abundance mindset is a belief system rooted in the belief that there is more than enough for everyone. It involves shifting from a scarcity mindset, which focuses on limitations and lack, to a mindset of abundance, which emphasizes abundance, possibility, and gratitude. Individuals with an abundance mindset approach life with optimism, confidence, and a sense of empowerment, knowing that they have the resources and capabilities to create the life they desire.

Benefits of Abundance Mindset:

Increased Resilience: People with an abundance mindset are more resilient in the face of challenges and setbacks. Instead of viewing obstacles as insurmountable barriers, they see them as opportunities for growth and learning.

Enhanced Creativity: Abundance mindset fosters creativity and innovation by encouraging individuals to explore new ideas, take calculated risks, and think outside the box. This creative thinking can lead to breakthroughs and new opportunities for success.

Greater Generosity: When you believe in abundance, you're more likely to share your resources, time, and talents with others. Acts of generosity and kindness not only benefit those around you but also create a positive ripple effect in your own life.

Attracting Opportunities: By maintaining a positive outlook and expecting the best, individuals with an abundance mindset attract opportunities, connections, and resources into their lives. Their positive energy and confidence draw others towards them, opening doors to new possibilities.

Improved Well-being: Cultivating an abundance mindset promotes feelings of gratitude, fulfillment, and satisfaction. By focusing on what you have rather than what you lack, you can experience greater overall well-being and happiness.

Strategies for Developing Wealth Consciousness:

Practice Gratitude: Start each day by expressing gratitude for the abundance in your life, whether it's your health, relationships, or opportunities. Keep a gratitude journal or take a few moments each day to reflect on the blessings in your life.

Visualize Success: Use visualization techniques to imagine yourself achieving your goals and living a life of abundance. Visualize the details of your ideal life, including your career, finances, relationships, and lifestyle. This practice can help align your thoughts and actions with your desired outcomes.

Affirmations: Create positive affirmations that reinforce abundance and wealth consciousness. Repeat these affirmations daily to reprogram your subconscious mind and reinforce positive beliefs about money, success, and abundance.

Surround Yourself with Positivity: Surround yourself with people who uplift and inspire you. Limit exposure to negative influences and seek out environments that foster growth, positivity, and abundance.

Invest in Self-Development: Continuously invest in your personal and professional development to expand your knowledge, skills, and capabilities. Attend seminars, workshops, or online courses that align with your goals and interests.

Take Inspired Action: Cultivate a proactive mindset and take inspired action towards your goals. Break down your goals into manageable steps and consistently work towards them with determination and focus.

Release Limiting Beliefs: Identify and release any limiting beliefs or negative thought patterns that may be holding you back from experiencing abundance. Replace these beliefs with empowering affirmations and beliefs that support your vision of success.

Embracing Abundance:

In conclusion, developing a mindset of abundance and wealth consciousness is a powerful catalyst for personal and financial growth. By embracing abundance, you can unlock your full potential, attract opportunities, and create a life of fulfillment and prosperity. Remember that abundance is not just about material wealth; it encompasses all aspects of life, including health, happiness, and relationships. By cultivating an abundance mindset and taking inspired action towards your goals, you can manifest your dreams and create a legacy of impact and abundance for generations to come.

6. Maximizing Wealth Growth: Leveraging Tax-Efficient Strategies

Taxes are a significant expense that can erode investment returns and hinder wealth accumulation. However, savvy investors understand that proactive tax planning and strategic decision-making can minimize tax liabilities and optimize wealth growth over the long term. By leveraging tax-efficient strategies, investors can keep more of their hard-earned money working for them, ultimately accelerating their journey towards financial independence. In this article, we'll explore the importance of tax efficiency, common tax-saving strategies, and practical tips for maximizing wealth growth while minimizing tax burdens.

The Importance of Tax Efficiency:

Tax efficiency refers to the ability to minimize taxes on investment income, capital gains, and distributions. It involves structuring investments and financial decisions in a way that maximizes after-tax returns while complying with tax laws and regulations. By prioritizing tax efficiency, investors can preserve more of their wealth, compound returns more effectively, and achieve their financial goals faster.

Common Tax-Efficient Strategies:

Utilize Tax-Advantaged Accounts: Take full advantage of tax-advantaged accounts such as Individual Retirement Accounts

(IRAs), 401(k)s, and Health Savings Accounts (HSAs). Contributions to these accounts may be tax-deductible or grow tax-deferred, allowing investments to compound without immediate tax implications.

Harvest Tax Losses: Implement tax-loss harvesting strategies to offset capital gains and minimize taxes on investment gains. By selling investments that have experienced losses and reinvesting the proceeds in similar but not identical securities, investors can realize tax benefits while maintaining portfolio diversification.

Invest in Tax-Efficient Funds: Choose tax-efficient investment vehicles such as index funds or exchange-traded funds (ETFs) that have low turnover and minimal capital gains distributions. These funds typically generate fewer taxable events, resulting in lower tax liabilities for investors.

Consider Municipal Bonds: Invest in municipal bonds, which offer tax-exempt interest income at the federal or state level, depending on the issuer's location. Municipal bonds can provide steady income with favorable tax treatment, particularly for investors in higher tax brackets.

Strategic Asset Location: Allocate investments across taxable and tax-advantaged accounts strategically to optimize tax efficiency. Place tax-inefficient assets, such as bonds or actively managed funds, in tax-advantaged accounts, while holding tax-efficient assets, such as equities, in taxable accounts.

Optimize Retirement Withdrawals: Plan retirement withdrawals strategically to minimize tax liabilities and maximize after-tax income. Consider factors such as tax brackets, required minimum distributions (RMDs), and Social Security benefits when determining the most tax-efficient withdrawal strategy.

Use Tax-Efficient Investment Strategies: Implement tax-efficient investment strategies such as buy-and-hold investing, which minimizes capital gains taxes by reducing portfolio turnover. Additionally, consider tax-deferred or tax-free investment options, such as Roth IRAs or 529 college savings plans, to maximize after-tax returns.

Practical Tips for Maximizing Tax Efficiency:

Stay Informed: Stay updated on changes to tax laws and regulations that may impact your investment strategy. Consult with a tax professional or financial advisor to ensure you're making informed decisions and taking advantage of available tax-saving opportunities.

Plan Ahead: Incorporate tax considerations into your financial planning process and proactively seek out tax-efficient strategies that align with your goals and risk tolerance. Start tax planning early in the year to capitalize on available tax-saving opportunities.

Monitor Tax Efficiency: Regularly review your investment portfolio and tax situation to identify opportunities for tax optimization.

Consider rebalancing your portfolio or implementing tax-saving strategies as needed to maintain tax efficiency over time.

Diversify Tax Strategies: Diversify your tax-saving strategies to spread risk and maximize benefits. Instead of relying on a single tax-saving technique, explore a combination of strategies that address different aspects of your financial plan and tax situation.

Stay Disciplined: Stick to your long-term investment strategy and resist the temptation to make impulsive decisions based solely on tax considerations. Maintain a disciplined approach to investing and tax planning, focusing on your overall financial objectives and risk tolerance.

Conclusion:

Tax-efficient investing is a critical component of wealth management that can significantly impact investment outcomes and financial success. By implementing tax-efficient strategies, investors can minimize tax liabilities, preserve more of their wealth, and accelerate wealth growth over time. Whether it's maximizing contributions to tax-advantaged accounts, harvesting tax losses, or strategically allocating assets, proactive tax planning can unlock opportunities for greater financial security and prosperity. Remember, tax efficiency is not a one-time effort but an ongoing process that requires vigilance, adaptability, and a commitment to optimizing after-tax returns. By prioritizing tax efficiency and incorporating tax-saving strategies into your investment approach, you can maximize wealth growth and achieve your long-term financial goals with confidence and peace of mind.

7. Building Multiple Streams of Passive Income: A Path to Financial Security

In today's dynamic economy, securing financial stability requires more than just relying on a single source of income. Building multiple streams of passive income offers a strategic approach to diversifying revenue sources, reducing reliance on traditional employment, and achieving long-term financial security. Passive income streams generate revenue with minimal ongoing effort or active involvement, allowing individuals to earn money while focusing on other pursuits or enjoying a greater work-life balance. In this article, we'll explore the importance of passive income, strategies for creating multiple streams of passive income, and the benefits of achieving financial security through diversification.

Understanding Passive Income:

Passive income is income generated from activities in which the individual is not materially involved, such as rental properties, dividend-paying stocks, royalties from intellectual property, and interest from savings or investments. Unlike active income, which requires ongoing time and effort to earn, passive income streams continue to generate revenue with limited or no direct involvement once established. While building passive income streams often requires upfront investment of time, money, or resources, the potential benefits in terms of financial freedom and flexibility are substantial.

Importance of Passive Income:

Diversification: Relying solely on a single source of income, such as employment, leaves individuals vulnerable to financial instability in the event of job loss, economic downturns, or unexpected expenses. Passive income streams provide diversification, spreading risk across multiple revenue sources and reducing dependence on any one source for financial support.

Resilience: Passive income streams offer resilience against economic volatility and market fluctuations. Even during periods of uncertainty or adversity, passive income continues to flow, providing a steady source of revenue and stability.

Financial Independence: Building multiple streams of passive income can pave the way to financial independence, allowing individuals to achieve their desired lifestyle without being tied to a traditional job or employer. Passive income provides the freedom to pursue personal interests, travel, spend time with family, or pursue entrepreneurial ventures on your own terms.

Wealth Accumulation: Passive income streams have the potential to generate wealth over time through compounding, reinvestment, and appreciation. As passive income grows, individuals can reinvest earnings into additional income-producing assets, accelerating wealth accumulation and long-term financial goals.

Strategies for Creating Multiple Streams of Passive Income:

Real Estate Investments: Investing in rental properties, commercial real estate, or real estate investment trusts (REITs) can generate passive income through rental payments, property appreciation, and tax benefits such as depreciation deductions.

Dividend-Paying Stocks: Investing in dividend-paying stocks or dividend-focused mutual funds provides passive income in the form of regular dividend payments. Dividends are typically paid quarterly or annually and can supplement income from other sources.

Interest-Bearing Investments: Savings accounts, certificates of deposit (CDs), bonds, and peer-to-peer lending platforms offer opportunities to earn passive income through interest payments. While interest rates may vary, these investments provide a predictable source of income over time.

Digital Products and Intellectual Property: Creating and selling digital products such as e-books, online courses, software, or digital artwork allows individuals to generate passive income from royalties or licensing fees. Intellectual property can provide ongoing revenue with minimal maintenance or overhead costs.

Affiliate Marketing: Partnering with companies as an affiliate marketer allows individuals to earn passive income by promoting products or services and earning commissions on sales or referrals. Affiliate marketing can be done through blogs, websites, social media platforms, or email marketing campaigns.

Peer-to-Peer Lending: Participating in peer-to-peer lending platforms enables individuals to earn passive income by lending money to borrowers in exchange for interest payments. While there are risks involved, peer-to-peer lending can provide attractive returns compared to traditional savings accounts or bonds.

Create and Monetize Content: Building a following on platforms such as YouTube, podcasts, or blogs allows individuals to monetize their content through advertising, sponsorships, memberships, or merchandise sales. Content creators can generate passive income by leveraging their audience and creating valuable, evergreen content.

Benefits of Achieving Financial Security through Diversification:

Stability and Peace of Mind: Diversifying income streams provides stability and peace of mind, knowing that you have multiple sources of revenue supporting your financial well-being. Even if one stream temporarily falters, others can continue to provide income and support.

Flexibility and Freedom: Achieving financial security through passive income affords individuals greater flexibility and freedom to pursue their passions, interests, and goals. Whether it's traveling, spending time with family, or pursuing entrepreneurial ventures, passive income allows for greater autonomy and control over one's time and lifestyle.

Long-Term Wealth Accumulation: Building multiple streams of passive income lays the foundation for long-term wealth accumulation and financial independence. As passive income grows and compounds over time, individuals can reinvest earnings, diversify investments, and achieve their financial goals more rapidly.

Resilience to Economic Uncertainty: Diversified income streams provide resilience against economic uncertainty, job loss, or market downturns. By spreading risk across multiple revenue sources, individuals can weather financial challenges more effectively and maintain financial stability in any economic climate.

Conclusion:

Building multiple streams of passive income is a strategic approach to achieving financial security, independence, and freedom. By diversifying income sources and leveraging opportunities for passive income generation, individuals can reduce reliance on traditional employment, create sustainable wealth, and enjoy greater flexibility and autonomy in their lives. Whether it's through real estate investments, dividend-paying stocks, digital products, or affiliate marketing, there are countless opportunities to generate passive income and create a brighter financial future. Start today by exploring different income streams, investing in assets that align with your goals, and taking steps towards building a diversified portfolio of passive income sources. With dedication, perseverance, and a commitment to financial growth, you can unlock the power of passive income and achieve your dreams of financial security and abundance.

8. Leveraging Debt for Wealth: Using Debt Wisely to Invest in Assets

Debt is often viewed as a financial burden, but when used strategically, it can be a powerful tool for building wealth and achieving financial goals. By leveraging debt to invest in income-producing assets, individuals can amplify returns, accelerate wealth accumulation, and create opportunities for long-term financial success. In this article, we'll explore the concept of leveraging debt, strategies for using debt wisely, and the potential benefits and risks of this approach.

Understanding Leveraged Investing:

Leveraged investing involves using borrowed funds, typically in the form of loans or margin accounts, to invest in assets with the potential to generate higher returns than the cost of borrowing. The goal is to amplify investment returns and accelerate wealth growth by magnifying the impact of invested capital. Common examples of leveraged investing include purchasing real estate with a mortgage, buying stocks on margin, or using loans to finance business ventures or acquisitions.

Strategies for Using Debt Wisely:

Invest in Income-Producing Assets: Use debt to invest in assets that have the potential to generate positive cash flow or appreciation over time. Examples include rental properties, dividend-paying stocks, bonds, and business ventures with strong revenue-generating potential.

Maintain Positive Cash Flow: Ensure that the income generated from your investments exceeds the cost of borrowing, including interest payments and any associated expenses. Positive cash flow provides a buffer against unexpected expenses or fluctuations in investment returns.

Diversify Investments: Spread borrowed funds across a diversified portfolio of assets to mitigate risk and optimize returns. Diversification helps minimize the impact of any single investment underperforming or experiencing losses.

Consider Tax Implications: Evaluate the tax implications of leveraged investments, including deductibility of interest payments and capital gains taxes. Consult with a tax professional to understand how leveraging debt may impact your overall tax liability and investment strategy.

Manage Risk: Assess your risk tolerance and ability to withstand market volatility or changes in interest rates. Consider factors such as loan terms, interest rates, and potential fluctuations in asset values when evaluating the suitability of leveraged investments for your financial situation.

Monitor and Rebalance: Regularly review your leveraged investments and adjust your strategy as needed based on changes in market conditions, interest rates, or personal financial goals. Rebalancing may involve refinancing debt, selling assets, or reallocating capital to maintain alignment with your investment objectives.

Benefits of Leveraging Debt:

Amplified Returns: Leveraged investing has the potential to magnify investment returns by allowing individuals to control a larger pool of assets with a relatively small amount of their own capital. By maximizing the use of borrowed funds, investors can capitalize on opportunities for growth and wealth accumulation.

Asset Accumulation: Leveraged investing enables individuals to acquire assets that may be otherwise out of reach due to limited capital. By leveraging debt, individuals can access real estate, stocks, or business opportunities that have the potential to appreciate in value and generate long-term wealth.

Diversification: Using debt to invest in a diversified portfolio of assets can spread risk and enhance overall investment performance. Diversification helps mitigate the impact of market volatility and provides a cushion against potential losses in any single investment.

Tax Benefits: Interest payments on certain types of debt, such as mortgage interest on investment properties or margin interest on investment accounts, may be tax-deductible. Leveraging debt can provide tax advantages that enhance overall after-tax returns on investment.

Risks and Considerations:

Interest Rate Risk: Changes in interest rates can impact the cost of borrowing and the affordability of debt payments. Rising interest rates may increase borrowing costs and reduce investment returns, while falling interest rates may increase the attractiveness of leveraged investments.

Market Volatility: Leveraged investments are subject to market volatility and fluctuations in asset prices. Market downturns or adverse economic conditions can amplify losses and increase the risk of default on debt obligations.

Liquidity Risk: In some cases, leveraged investments may be illiquid or difficult to sell, especially during periods of market distress. Illiquid investments can hinder the ability to access capital or refinance debt, potentially leading to financial strain.

Debt Serviceability: Assess your ability to service debt payments, including interest and principal, under various scenarios. Consider factors such as rental income, dividend yields, and business cash flow when evaluating the feasibility of leveraged investments.

Conclusion:

Leveraging debt for wealth-building purposes can be a powerful strategy for accelerating investment growth and achieving financial goals. By using borrowed funds to invest in income-producing assets, individuals can amplify returns, diversify portfolios, and access opportunities for long-term wealth accumulation. However, leveraging debt also involves risks and considerations that require careful planning, evaluation, and risk management. It's essential to assess your risk tolerance, financial situation, and investment objectives before embarking on a leveraged investing strategy. With prudent planning, disciplined execution, and a focus on long-term financial success, leveraging debt wisely can be a valuable tool for building wealth and achieving financial independence.

9. Investing in Assets with Intrinsic Value: Exploring Real Estate and Precious Metals

In an ever-changing financial landscape, investors seek assets with intrinsic value to protect and grow their wealth over time. Real estate and precious metals are two prominent examples of tangible assets that have stood the test of time as stores of value and vehicles for wealth preservation. In this article, we'll delve into the reasons for investing in real estate and precious metals, the unique characteristics of each asset class, and strategies for incorporating them into an investment portfolio.

Real Estate: A Time-Tested Investment Vehicle

Real estate has long been regarded as a cornerstone of wealth building and financial security. Unlike stocks or bonds, which derive their value from market speculation and investor sentiment, real estate offers tangible benefits and intrinsic value that endure over time. Here are some compelling reasons to consider investing in real estate:

Income Generation: One of the primary attractions of real estate investment is the potential for rental income. Owning rental properties allows investors to generate passive cash flow, which can provide a steady stream of income to support living expenses or reinvestment.

Appreciation Potential: In addition to rental income, real estate investments have the potential to appreciate in value over time. Demand for real estate tends to increase with population growth and economic development, driving property prices higher and enhancing overall investment returns.

Hedge Against Inflation: Real estate is often considered a hedge against inflation, as property values and rental income tend to rise in tandem with inflationary pressures. By owning tangible assets with intrinsic value, investors can preserve purchasing power and mitigate the erosion of wealth caused by rising prices.

Portfolio Diversification: Including real estate in an investment portfolio provides diversification benefits, as real estate returns have historically exhibited low correlation with those of stocks and bonds. Diversification helps reduce overall portfolio volatility and enhances risk-adjusted returns.

Tax Advantages: Real estate investors may benefit from various tax advantages, including depreciation deductions, mortgage interest deductions, and capital gains tax deferral through like-kind exchanges. These tax incentives can enhance after-tax returns and improve overall investment performance.

Precious Metals: A Safe Haven in Times of Uncertainty

Precious metals, such as gold and silver, have been valued throughout history for their rarity, durability, and intrinsic worth. Investors turn to precious metals as a safe haven during times of economic uncertainty and market volatility. Here are some reasons why investors choose to invest in precious metals:

Store of Value: Precious metals have served as a reliable store of value for thousands of years, preserving wealth through periods of political upheaval, currency devaluation, and economic crisis. Gold, in particular, is often viewed as a hedge against currency depreciation and financial instability.

41

Portfolio Diversification: Including precious metals in an investment portfolio provides diversification benefits, as precious metals prices have historically exhibited low correlation with those of traditional asset classes such as stocks and bonds. Precious metals can help offset losses during market downturns and enhance overall portfolio resilience.

Inflation Protection: Precious metals are often seen as a hedge against inflation, as their intrinsic value tends to rise in response to inflationary pressures. During periods of high inflation or currency debasement, investors flock to precious metals as a store of value and a means of preserving purchasing power.

Liquidity: Precious metals are highly liquid assets that can be easily bought, sold, and traded in global markets. Gold and silver bullion, coins, and exchange-traded funds (ETFs) provide investors with convenient access to the precious metals market, allowing for seamless portfolio management and risk mitigation.

Safe Haven Appeal: Precious metals have a unique safe-haven appeal during times of geopolitical tension, financial instability, or market turmoil. Investors turn to gold and silver as a refuge from market uncertainty, seeking the stability and security offered by these timeless assets.

Incorporating Real Estate and Precious Metals into an Investment Portfolio:

Strategic Allocation: Determine the appropriate allocation of real estate and precious metals within your investment portfolio based on your risk tolerance, investment objectives, and time horizon. Consider factors such as asset class correlation, liquidity needs, and portfolio diversification goals when determining allocation percentages.

Diversification: Ensure that your investment portfolio is well-diversified across asset classes, including equities, fixed income, real estate, precious metals, and alternative investments. Diversification helps spread risk and reduces the impact of individual asset class fluctuations on overall portfolio performance.

Risk Management: Assess the risks associated with investing in real estate and precious metals, including market volatility, liquidity constraints, and geopolitical factors. Implement risk management strategies such as position sizing, stop-loss orders, and hedging techniques to mitigate potential losses and preserve capital.

Due Diligence: Conduct thorough due diligence before investing in real estate or precious metals. Research market trends, supply and demand dynamics, regulatory considerations, and investment fundamentals to make informed investment decisions and minimize risks.

Regular Monitoring: Monitor the performance of your real estate and precious metals investments regularly and adjust your portfolio allocation as needed based on changing market conditions, economic outlook, and investment objectives. Stay informed about developments in the real estate market, precious metals market, and global economy to make timely adjustments to your investment strategy.

Conclusion:

Investing in assets with intrinsic value, such as real estate and precious metals, offers investors unique opportunities for wealth preservation, portfolio diversification, and risk management. Real estate provides the potential for rental income, property appreciation, and tax advantages, while precious metals serve as a safe haven during times of economic uncertainty and inflationary pressures. By incorporating real estate and precious metals into an investment portfolio strategically, investors can enhance overall portfolio resilience, mitigate risk, and achieve long-term financial goals with confidence and peace of mind. Whether it's through direct ownership of properties, real estate investment trusts (REITs), gold bullion, or precious metals ETFs, investors have a variety of options for accessing these valuable asset classes and positioning their portfolios for success in any market environment.

10. Unleashing the Power of Entrepreneurship: A Path to Wealth Creation

Entrepreneurship has long been heralded as a catalyst for innovation, economic growth, and societal change. Beyond its transformative impact on industries and markets, entrepreneurship offers individuals a unique opportunity to create wealth, achieve financial independence, and leave a lasting legacy. In this article, we'll explore the potential of entrepreneurship for wealth creation, the characteristics of successful entrepreneurs, and practical strategies for aspiring business owners to harness the power of entrepreneurship on their journey to prosperity.

The Promise of Entrepreneurship:

Entrepreneurship embodies the spirit of creativity, resilience, and risk-taking that drives progress and prosperity in economies around the world. Unlike traditional employment, which offers limited income potential and relies on the exchange of time for money, entrepreneurship empowers individuals to create value, solve problems, and build wealth on their own terms. Here are some reasons why entrepreneurship holds such promise for wealth creation:

Unlimited Income Potential: Unlike salaried employment, where income is typically capped by salary scales or hourly rates, entrepreneurship offers unlimited income potential. Successful entrepreneurs have the ability to scale their businesses, leverage technology, and innovate new revenue streams, leading to exponential growth and wealth accumulation.

Ownership and Control: As business owners, entrepreneurs have the autonomy to make decisions, set priorities, and chart their own course towards success. By owning equity in their businesses, entrepreneurs can capture the full value created by their efforts and retain control over their destiny.

Opportunity for Innovation: Entrepreneurship is a breeding ground for innovation, disruption, and groundbreaking ideas. Entrepreneurs have the freedom to pursue their passions, experiment with new business models, and pioneer solutions to pressing societal challenges, creating value and wealth in the process.

Job Creation and Economic Impact: Successful entrepreneurs not only create wealth for themselves but also generate employment opportunities, stimulate economic growth, and drive positive change within their communities. By building successful businesses, entrepreneurs contribute to job creation, wealth distribution, and the overall prosperity of society.

Legacy Building: Entrepreneurship offers the opportunity to leave a lasting legacy and impact future generations. By building sustainable businesses, nurturing talent, and fostering innovation, entrepreneurs can create enduring wealth and influence that transcends individual lifetimes.

Characteristics of Successful Entrepreneurs:

While entrepreneurship offers immense potential for wealth creation, not everyone is cut out to be a successful entrepreneur. Successful entrepreneurs possess a unique set of characteristics, skills, and mindsets that enable them to thrive in the competitive business landscape. Here are some key traits of successful entrepreneurs:

Visionary Leadership: Successful entrepreneurs have a clear vision of their goals, aspirations, and the impact they want to make in the world. They possess the ability to inspire others, communicate their vision effectively, and rally support behind their ideas.

Resilience and Perseverance: Entrepreneurship is fraught with challenges, setbacks, and failures. Successful entrepreneurs possess resilience, grit, and perseverance to overcome obstacles, learn from failure, and keep pushing forward in the face of adversity.

Adaptability and Flexibility: The business landscape is constantly evolving, requiring entrepreneurs to adapt to changing market conditions, consumer preferences, and technological advancements. Successful entrepreneurs are nimble, flexible, and open-minded, willing to pivot their strategies and embrace new opportunities as they arise.

Risk-Taking and Courage: Entrepreneurship inherently involves risk, uncertainty, and the willingness to step outside of one's comfort zone. Successful entrepreneurs are comfortable taking calculated risks, making tough decisions, and embracing failure as part of the learning process.

Passion and Purpose: Passion fuels entrepreneurship, driving individuals to pursue their dreams, overcome obstacles, and persist in the face of challenges. Successful entrepreneurs are deeply passionate about their work, driven by a sense of purpose, and committed to making a positive impact in the world.

Strategies for Harnessing Entrepreneurship for Wealth Creation:

Identify Opportunities: Look for unmet needs, underserved markets, or areas ripe for disruption. Conduct market research, analyze trends, and identify opportunities for innovation and value creation.

Validate Your Idea: Test your business idea by conducting market validation, gathering feedback from potential customers, and assessing demand for your product or service. Validate your assumptions, refine your value proposition, and ensure there is a viable market for your offering.

Build a Strong Team: Surround yourself with talented individuals who complement your skills, expertise, and vision. Build a strong team culture, foster collaboration, and empower your team members to contribute their unique talents to the success of the business.

Execute with Excellence: Focus on execution and implementation, turning your vision into reality through strategic planning, disciplined execution, and attention to detail. Set clear goals, establish key performance indicators (KPIs), and track progress towards achieving your objectives.

Embrace Innovation: Continuously innovate and adapt to stay ahead of the competition and capitalize on emerging trends. Embrace technology, explore new business models, and remain agile in response to changes in the market landscape.

Manage Finances Wisely: Practice sound financial management, budgeting, and cash flow forecasting to ensure the sustainability and profitability of your business. Monitor expenses, control costs, and reinvest profits strategically to fuel growth and expansion.

Seek Mentorship and Guidance: Surround yourself with mentors, advisors, and peers who can provide guidance, support, and valuable insights as you navigate the entrepreneurial journey. Learn from the experiences of others, seek advice from seasoned entrepreneurs, and leverage networks for opportunities and resources.

Conclusion:

Entrepreneurship holds immense potential for wealth creation, financial independence, and personal fulfillment. By harnessing the power of entrepreneurship, individuals can create value, solve meaningful problems, and build businesses that generate lasting wealth and impact. Whether it's through innovative startups, scalable ventures, or legacy-building enterprises, entrepreneurship offers a path to prosperity and success for those willing to embrace the challenges and opportunities of the entrepreneurial journey. With vision, resilience, and a commitment to excellence, aspiring entrepreneurs can unleash their potential, create wealth, and leave a lasting legacy for generations to come.

11. Implementing Strategies for Wealth Preservation and Intergenerational Wealth Transfer

Wealth preservation and intergenerational wealth transfer are essential components of comprehensive financial planning aimed at safeguarding assets, ensuring financial security for future generations, and leaving a lasting legacy. As individuals accumulate wealth over their lifetimes, it becomes increasingly important to implement strategies that protect and grow assets while effectively transferring wealth to heirs and beneficiaries. In this article, we'll explore the importance of wealth preservation and intergenerational wealth transfer, common challenges and considerations, and practical strategies for preserving wealth and facilitating seamless wealth transfer across generations.

The Importance of Wealth Preservation and Intergenerational Wealth Transfer:

Wealth preservation involves safeguarding assets and maintaining their value over time, while intergenerational wealth transfer focuses on passing assets from one generation to the next in a tax-efficient and equitable manner. Both aspects are critical for ensuring the long-term financial well-being of individuals and their families. Here's why wealth preservation and intergenerational wealth transfer are important:

Maintaining Financial Security: Wealth preservation ensures that individuals can maintain their desired standard of living and meet their financial goals throughout their lifetimes. By protecting assets from erosion due to inflation, market volatility, and unforeseen expenses, wealth preservation provides a foundation for financial security and peace of mind.

Preserving Family Legacy: Intergenerational wealth transfer allows individuals to pass down their values, beliefs, and traditions along with their financial assets. By preserving family legacy and heritage, wealth transfer fosters a sense of continuity, identity, and connection across generations.

Supporting Future Generations: Effective wealth transfer enables individuals to provide for the needs and aspirations of their descendants, whether it's funding education, supporting entrepreneurial ventures, or ensuring access to quality healthcare. By empowering future generations with financial resources, wealth transfer creates opportunities for personal growth, achievement, and success.

Minimizing Tax Liabilities: Thoughtful estate planning and wealth transfer strategies can help minimize tax liabilities and maximize the value of assets passed to heirs and beneficiaries. By leveraging tax-efficient vehicles and structures, individuals can reduce the impact of estate taxes, gift taxes, and capital gains taxes on their estates.

Promoting Family Harmony: Properly executed wealth transfer plans can help prevent disputes, conflicts, and misunderstandings among family members. By transparently communicating intentions, managing expectations, and establishing clear guidelines for asset distribution, individuals can promote harmony and unity within their families.

Challenges and Considerations:

While wealth preservation and intergenerational wealth transfer offer numerous benefits, they also present challenges and considerations that must be addressed. Some common challenges include:

Complexity of Estate Planning: Estate planning can be complex and multifaceted, involving legal, financial, and tax considerations. Individuals must navigate a variety of estate planning tools and strategies, such as wills, trusts, powers of attorney, and beneficiary designations, to effectively manage their estates.

Family Dynamics: Family dynamics, relationships, and communication patterns can impact the success of wealth transfer initiatives. Disagreements, conflicts, and competing interests among family members may complicate the estate planning process and strain intergenerational relationships.

Tax Implications: Tax laws and regulations governing estate and gift taxes are subject to change and vary by jurisdiction. Individuals must stay informed about relevant tax laws and consult with tax professionals to develop tax-efficient wealth transfer strategies that align with their objectives.

Asset Protection: Protecting assets from creditors, lawsuits, and other potential threats is essential for preserving wealth over the long term. Individuals may need to implement asset protection strategies, such as establishing trusts or limited liability entities, to shield assets from risks and liabilities.

Succession Planning: In the case of family-owned businesses or closely held assets, succession planning is crucial for ensuring a smooth transition of ownership and management to the next generation. Succession planning involves identifying successors, grooming future leaders, and implementing strategies for business continuity and growth.

Strategies for Wealth Preservation and Intergenerational Wealth Transfer:

Comprehensive Estate Planning: Develop a comprehensive estate plan that addresses your unique circumstances, goals, and preferences. Work with estate planning professionals, such as attorneys, financial advisors, and tax specialists, to create wills, trusts, and other legal documents that reflect your wishes and protect your assets.

Asset Allocation and Diversification: Implement a disciplined investment strategy that emphasizes asset allocation and diversification to manage risk and preserve capital. Spread investments across a mix of asset classes, such as stocks, bonds, real estate, and alternative investments, to mitigate volatility and optimize returns over time.

Lifetime Giving: Consider making lifetime gifts to heirs and beneficiaries to reduce estate taxes and facilitate wealth transfer while you're still alive. Utilize annual gift tax exclusions, lifetime gift tax exemptions, and tax-efficient gifting strategies to transfer assets to loved ones and charities.

Use of Trusts: Explore the use of trusts as powerful estate planning tools for wealth preservation and intergenerational wealth transfer. Establish irrevocable trusts, revocable living trusts, charitable trusts, and other trust structures to achieve specific objectives, such as asset protection, tax

12. Cultivating Financial Discipline and Resilience Amid Market Volatility

Financial discipline and resilience are essential virtues for navigating the ups and downs of the financial markets with confidence and composure. In an environment marked by volatility, uncertainty, and unexpected events, cultivating these qualities can empower individuals to make sound financial decisions, stay focused on their long-term goals, and weather market turbulence with resilience. In this article, we'll explore the importance of financial discipline and resilience, practical strategies for developing these attributes, and ways to stay resilient in the face of market volatility.

The Importance of Financial Discipline and Resilience:

Financial discipline and resilience serve as pillars of financial well-being, providing individuals with the strength, determination, and self-control needed to achieve their financial goals and withstand adversity. Here's why these qualities are crucial:

Maintaining Focus on Long-Term Goals: Financial discipline helps individuals stay focused on their long-term goals and resist the temptation to make impulsive decisions based on short-term market fluctuations. By maintaining a disciplined approach to saving, investing, and spending, individuals can stay on track towards achieving their financial aspirations.

Building Wealth Over Time: Consistent saving and investing behaviors, supported by financial discipline, are key drivers of wealth accumulation over time. By adhering to a disciplined savings plan, avoiding unnecessary debt, and making prudent investment choices, individuals can build a solid financial foundation and create opportunities for long-term prosperity.

Managing Financial Risks: Financial resilience enables individuals to manage financial risks and withstand unexpected events, such as job loss, illness, or economic downturns. By maintaining an emergency fund, having adequate insurance coverage, and diversifying investments, individuals can mitigate the impact of adverse circumstances and bounce back from setbacks more effectively.

Embracing Market Volatility: Financial resilience empowers individuals to embrace market volatility as a natural part of the investment process and avoid reactionary behavior in response to short-term market movements. By staying disciplined and focused on their investment strategy, individuals can capitalize on opportunities presented by market fluctuations and avoid making emotional decisions that may undermine their long-term success.

Practical Strategies for Cultivating Financial Discipline and Resilience:

Set Clear Financial Goals: Define your financial goals, both short-term and long-term, and establish a roadmap for achieving them. Break down your goals into actionable steps, set measurable targets, and track your progress regularly to stay motivated and accountable.

Create a Budget and Stick to It: Develop a realistic budget that aligns with your financial goals and priorities, and commit to sticking to it consistently. Track your income, expenses, and savings diligently, and make adjustments as needed to ensure that your spending remains in line with your financial plan.

Automate Savings and Investments: Set up automatic transfers from your checking account to your savings or investment accounts to ensure that you consistently save and invest a portion of your income each month. By automating your contributions, you remove the temptation to spend impulsively and reinforce positive saving habits.

Practice Delayed Gratification: Cultivate the habit of delaying gratification and avoiding unnecessary impulse purchases. Before making a significant financial decision, take the time to consider the long-term implications and weigh the trade-offs between immediate satisfaction and future financial security.

Stay Informed and Educated: Continuously educate yourself about personal finance, investing principles, and market dynamics to make informed decisions and build confidence in your financial capabilities. Stay abreast of current events, economic trends, and changes in tax laws or regulations that may impact your financial situation.

Build a Support Network: Surround yourself with supportive friends, family members, or financial advisors who share your commitment to financial discipline and resilience. Seek guidance, feedback, and encouragement from trusted sources, and leverage their expertise to navigate financial challenges and stay on course towards your goals.

Maintaining Resilience in the Face of Market Volatility:

Focus on the Long Term: Maintain a long-term perspective and avoid getting caught up in short-term market fluctuations. Remember that investing is a marathon, not a sprint, and focus on the fundamentals of your investment strategy rather than reacting to daily market noise.

Diversify Your Investments: Diversification is a key risk management strategy that can help mitigate the impact of market volatility on your investment portfolio. Spread your investments across a mix of asset classes, sectors, and geographic regions to reduce concentration risk and enhance portfolio resilience.

Stay Calm and Avoid Emotional Decision-Making: During periods of market volatility, emotions can run high, leading to impulsive decisions that may undermine your long-term financial goals. Stay calm, rational, and disciplined in your approach to investing, and avoid making knee-jerk reactions based on fear or greed.

Rebalance Your Portfolio Regularly: Periodically review and rebalance your investment portfolio to realign your asset allocation with your target allocation. Rebalancing helps ensure that your portfolio remains aligned with your risk tolerance and investment objectives, especially during periods of market volatility.

Focus on What You Can Control: While you can't control market fluctuations or macroeconomic events, you can control your response to them. Focus on factors within your control, such as your savings rate, investment strategy, and spending habits, and take proactive steps to manage your finances effectively.

Seek Professional Advice When Needed: If you're feeling overwhelmed or uncertain about how to navigate market volatility, don't hesitate to seek guidance from a financial advisor or investment professional. A qualified advisor can provide objective advice, perspective, and expertise to help you make informed decisions and stay on track towards your financial goals.

Conclusion:

Financial discipline and resilience are essential qualities for achieving financial success and security in an unpredictable world. By cultivating these virtues and implementing practical strategies for managing your finances effectively, you can build a solid foundation for long-term prosperity, withstand market volatility with confidence, and achieve your financial goals with resilience and determination. Whether you're saving for retirement, investing for the future, or planning for intergenerational wealth transfer, maintaining discipline and resilience will empower you to navigate life's financial challenges and seize opportunities for growth and prosperity.

13. Incorporating Philanthropy and Giving into Your Wealth Mastery Journey

Philanthropy and giving are integral components of a holistic approach to wealth mastery, providing individuals with opportunities to make a meaningful impact on their communities, society at large, and causes they care about deeply. Beyond financial success and material wealth, philanthropy offers individuals a sense of purpose, fulfillment, and social responsibility, enriching their lives and leaving a lasting legacy of generosity and compassion. In this article, we'll explore the importance of incorporating philanthropy and giving into your wealth mastery journey, the benefits of philanthropic activities, and practical strategies for making a positive difference in the world through charitable giving.

The Importance of Philanthropy and Giving:

Philanthropy encompasses acts of generosity, compassion, and altruism aimed at improving the well-being of others and addressing pressing societal challenges. Whether through financial contributions, volunteer work, or advocacy efforts, philanthropy plays a vital role in driving positive change and fostering social progress. Here's why incorporating philanthropy and giving into your wealth mastery journey is important:

Creating Meaning and Fulfillment: Philanthropy provides individuals with a sense of purpose, meaning, and fulfillment beyond material wealth. By giving back to others and making a difference in the lives of those less fortunate, individuals experience a profound sense of satisfaction and fulfillment that transcends financial success.

Making a Positive Impact: Philanthropy empowers individuals to address critical social issues, support causes they are passionate about, and drive positive change in their communities and the world. Through strategic giving and philanthropic initiatives, individuals can contribute to meaningful solutions to poverty, inequality, environmental degradation, and other pressing challenges.

Building Stronger Communities: Philanthropy strengthens the fabric of society by fostering a culture of giving, empathy, and collaboration. By supporting local nonprofits, community organizations, and grassroots initiatives, individuals can help build stronger, more resilient communities where everyone has the opportunity to thrive.

Inspiring Others to Give: Philanthropy has a ripple effect, inspiring others to join in the effort to make a difference. By leading by example and sharing their philanthropic journey with others, individuals can inspire friends, family members, and colleagues to get involved in charitable giving and amplify the impact of their collective efforts.

Leaving a Lasting Legacy: Philanthropy offers individuals the opportunity to leave a meaningful legacy that extends beyond their lifetime. By supporting causes they care about deeply and establishing charitable foundations or endowments, individuals can ensure that their values, beliefs, and aspirations continue to shape the world for generations to come.

The Benefits of Philanthropic Activities:

Engaging in philanthropic activities offers a wide range of benefits, both for the recipients of charitable support and for the individuals giving back. Some of the key benefits of philanthropy include:

Sense of Purpose and Fulfillment: Philanthropy provides individuals with a sense of purpose, fulfillment, and personal satisfaction derived from making a positive impact on the lives of others.

Enhanced Well-Being: Giving back has been shown to improve mental and emotional well-being, reduce stress, and increase happiness and life satisfaction.

Social Connection and Community Engagement: Philanthropy fosters social connection, empathy, and a sense of belonging by bringing people together around shared values and common causes.

Personal Growth and Development: Engaging in philanthropy can lead to personal growth, self-discovery, and expanded perspectives as individuals learn about pressing social issues and the needs of others.

Positive Reputation and Influence: Philanthropy enhances individuals' reputations and social standing by demonstrating their commitment to making a positive difference in the world and inspiring others to follow their lead.

Practical Strategies for Incorporating Philanthropy and Giving into Your Wealth Mastery Journey:

Define Your Values and Priorities: Identify causes, issues, or organizations that align with your values, interests, and priorities. Consider the impact you want to make and the legacy you want to leave through your philanthropic efforts.

Set Giving Goals: Establish specific giving goals and objectives based on your financial capacity, philanthropic vision, and desired impact. Determine how much you want to give, what causes you want to support, and how you plan to measure the success of your philanthropic initiatives.

Create a Philanthropic Plan: Develop a strategic philanthropic plan that outlines your giving strategy, target beneficiaries, and planned activities. Consider whether you want to make one-time donations, establish recurring giving programs, or create a charitable foundation or donor-advised fund.

Research and Due Diligence: Conduct thorough research and due diligence to identify reputable nonprofits, charities, or social enterprises that align with your philanthropic goals and have a track record of impact and effectiveness.

Maximize Impact Through Strategic Giving: Focus your philanthropic efforts on areas where you can make the greatest impact and leverage your resources most effectively. Consider funding high-impact interventions, supporting innovative solutions, or collaborating with other donors to amplify your collective impact.

Engage in Hands-On Volunteering: In addition to financial contributions, consider volunteering your time, skills, and expertise to support charitable organizations and community initiatives. Hands-on volunteering allows you to make a direct impact, build meaningful connections, and deepen your understanding of social issues.

Promote Transparency and Accountability: Prioritize transparency, accountability, and ethical stewardship in your philanthropic activities. Seek out organizations that demonstrate transparency in their operations, use funds efficiently, and regularly report on their impact and outcomes.

Involve Your Family and Loved Ones: Engage your family members, children, or loved ones in your philanthropic journey by involving them in decision-making, volunteering together, or establishing family giving traditions. Instilling the value of giving back in future generations ensures that your philanthropic legacy endures.

Conclusion:

Incorporating philanthropy and giving into your wealth mastery journey offers a powerful pathway to personal fulfillment, social impact, and lasting legacy. By embracing the principles of generosity, compassion, and social responsibility, individuals can make a meaningful difference in the lives of others, strengthen their communities, and leave a positive imprint on the world. Whether through financial contributions, volunteer work, advocacy efforts, or strategic partnerships, philanthropy provides individuals with the opportunity to leverage their resources, talents, and influence to create a brighter, more equitable future for all. As you embark on your philanthropic journey, remember that every act of kindness, no matter how small, has the power to make a difference and change lives for the better.

14. Navigating the Psychology of Money: Understanding Emotions and Biases

Money is not just a medium of exchange; it's deeply intertwined with our emotions, beliefs, and behaviors. The psychology of money explores how our thoughts, feelings, and biases influence our financial decisions, from spending and saving to investing and giving. By understanding the psychological factors that shape our relationship with money, we can make more informed decisions, avoid common pitfalls, and cultivate healthier financial habits. In this article, we'll delve into the psychology of money, explore key emotions and biases that affect our financial choices, and discuss practical strategies for navigating them effectively.

The Role of Emotions in Financial Decision-Making:

Emotions play a significant role in how we perceive, evaluate, and respond to financial situations. From fear and greed to joy and regret, our emotions can influence our financial decisions in profound ways. Here are some common emotions that impact our relationship with money:

Fear: Fear of loss or failure can lead to risk aversion, hesitancy to invest, and missed opportunities for growth. Fear-based decisions may result in overly conservative investment strategies, missed market rallies, or impulsive selling during market downturns.

Greed: Greed can tempt us to chase high-risk, high-reward investments, engage in speculative trading, or overspend beyond our means. Greed-driven behavior may lead to impulsive decisions, excessive risk-taking, and financial losses in pursuit of unrealistic gains.

Anxiety: Financial anxiety can arise from uncertainty about the future, mounting debt, or inadequate savings. Anxiety may manifest as indecision, procrastination, or avoidance of financial planning tasks, hindering our ability to take proactive steps to improve our financial situation.

Joy: The thrill of financial success, such as receiving a windfall or achieving investment gains, can evoke feelings of joy and satisfaction. While joy can be a positive motivator, it's essential to avoid letting euphoria cloud judgment or lead to reckless decision-making.

Regret: Regret over past financial decisions or missed opportunities can weigh heavily on our minds and influence future behavior. Dwelling on past mistakes may lead to avoidance of similar opportunities or reluctance to take calculated risks in the future.

Common Behavioral Biases in Financial Decision-Making:

In addition to emotions, cognitive biases—mental shortcuts or heuristics—can distort our perception of reality and influence our financial choices. These biases often lead to irrational or suboptimal decisions, despite our best intentions. Here are some common behavioral biases that affect financial decision-making:

Loss Aversion: Loss aversion refers to the tendency to prefer avoiding losses over acquiring equivalent gains. Loss aversion can lead to risk aversion, reluctance to sell losing investments, and holding onto underperforming assets in the hope of recovering losses.

Confirmation Bias: Confirmation bias is the tendency to seek out information that confirms our preexisting beliefs or opinions while ignoring or discounting contradictory evidence. Confirmation bias can lead to selective exposure to financial news, overconfidence in investment decisions, and resistance to alternative viewpoints.

Anchoring: Anchoring occurs when individuals rely too heavily on a specific reference point or initial piece of information when making decisions. Anchoring can lead to suboptimal price anchoring in negotiations, overvaluing past purchase prices, or fixating on historical investment returns.

Herding Behavior: Herding behavior involves following the crowd or mimicking the actions of others without independent analysis or critical thinking. Herding behavior can contribute to market bubbles, stock market crashes, and the propagation of financial fads or trends.

Overconfidence: Overconfidence bias occurs when individuals overestimate their knowledge, skills, or ability to predict future outcomes. Overconfidence can lead to excessive trading, speculative investments, and failure to adequately assess and manage risk.

Strategies for Navigating the Psychology of Money:

Cultivate Self-Awareness: Become aware of your emotions, biases, and psychological tendencies that influence your financial decisions. Practice mindfulness, reflection, and journaling to better understand your motivations, triggers, and patterns of behavior.

Establish Clear Goals: Set clear, measurable financial goals that align with your values, priorities, and aspirations. Having specific goals helps focus your attention, prioritize your spending and saving decisions, and resist impulsive urges.

Develop a Financial Plan: Create a comprehensive financial plan that outlines your income, expenses, savings, investments, and debt management strategies. A well-defined financial plan provides a roadmap for achieving your goals and serves as a guide during times of uncertainty or temptation.

Diversify Your Investments: Mitigate the impact of cognitive biases such as loss aversion and anchoring by diversifying your investment portfolio. Spread your investments across a mix of asset classes, sectors, and geographic regions to reduce concentration risk and enhance portfolio resilience.

Practice Rational Decision-Making: When faced with financial decisions, take a step back and evaluate the situation objectively. Avoid making impulsive decisions based on fear, greed, or other emotional impulses. Instead, gather relevant information, weigh the pros and cons, and consider the long-term consequences of your actions.

Seek Objective Advice: Consult with a financial advisor or trusted mentor who can provide objective, evidence-based guidance and help you avoid common behavioral pitfalls. An outside perspective can offer valuable insights, challenge your assumptions, and keep your financial decisions grounded in reality.

Set Boundaries and Limits: Establish clear boundaries and limits around your financial behaviors to prevent excessive risk-taking, overspending, or emotional decision-making. Implement safeguards, such as automatic savings plans or spending caps, to keep your financial habits in check.

Practice Gratitude and Contentment: Cultivate gratitude and contentment with what you have, rather than constantly striving for more. Recognize the abundance in your life, appreciate the non-material aspects of wealth, and focus on experiences that bring joy and fulfillment beyond monetary wealth.

Conclusion:

Understanding the psychology of money is essential for making informed, rational financial decisions and achieving long-term financial success. By recognizing the role of emotions and biases in shaping our financial behavior, we can develop strategies to mitigate their impact, cultivate healthier financial habits, and navigate the complexities of the financial landscape with greater confidence and resilience. Whether it's setting clear goals, diversifying investments, seeking objective advice, or practicing rational decision-making, incorporating psychological insights into our financial planning process empowers us to overcome cognitive biases, harness our emotions productively, and achieve our financial goals with clarity and purpose.

15. Mastering Negotiation Skills for Maximizing Income and Investment Opportunities

Negotiation skills are essential in various aspects of life, from business transactions and salary negotiations to investment deals and contractual agreements. Mastering negotiation skills not only helps you achieve favorable outcomes and maximize income but also enables you to capitalize on investment opportunities and build wealth over time. In this article, we'll explore the fundamentals of negotiation, key strategies for success, and practical tips for mastering negotiation skills to enhance your financial prospects and achieve your goals.

Understanding the Fundamentals of Negotiation:
Negotiation is a process of communication and compromise aimed at reaching mutually beneficial agreements between parties with conflicting interests or objectives. Whether you're negotiating a salary raise, a real estate purchase, or a business partnership, effective negotiation requires preparation, strategy, and communication skills. Here are some fundamental principles of negotiation to keep in mind:

Know Your Objectives: Clearly define your goals, priorities, and desired outcomes before entering into negotiations. Identify your non-negotiables and areas where you're willing to compromise to achieve a mutually acceptable agreement.

Understand Your Counterpart: Research and gather information about the other party's interests, needs, preferences, and constraints. Understanding your counterpart's perspective allows you to tailor your approach and propose solutions that address their concerns while advancing your own objectives.

Build Rapport: Establishing rapport and trust with the other party is essential for fostering open communication, cooperation, and collaboration. Listen actively, show empathy, and demonstrate a genuine interest in finding common ground to build a positive relationship and facilitate productive negotiations.

Focus on Value Creation: Instead of viewing negotiation as a zero-sum game where one party's gain is another's loss, adopt a mindset of value creation and mutual benefit. Look for opportunities to expand the pie and create value for both parties through creative problem-solving and innovative solutions.

Key Strategies for Successful Negotiation:
Prepare Thoroughly: Invest time and effort in thorough preparation before entering into negotiations. Research market conditions, gather relevant data and information, and anticipate potential objections or challenges to develop a well-informed negotiation strategy.

Set Realistic Expectations: Set realistic and achievable goals for the negotiation based on your objectives, alternatives, and the context of the situation. Avoid setting unrealistic expectations that may lead to disappointment or impede progress towards reaching a favorable agreement.

Focus on Interests, Not Positions: Instead of focusing solely on your own position or demands, focus on underlying interests, needs, and concerns shared by both parties. Identify common ground and explore win-win solutions that address mutual interests and create value for all stakeholders.

Communicate Effectively: Effective communication is critical in negotiation to convey your message clearly, assertively, and persuasively. Use active listening, ask probing questions, and seek clarification to ensure mutual understanding and avoid misunderstandings or misinterpretations.

Be Flexible and Adaptive: Flexibility and adaptability are key attributes of successful negotiators. Be willing to adjust your approach, explore alternative options, and make concessions when necessary to overcome impasses and keep negotiations moving forward towards a mutually acceptable outcome.

Manage Emotions: Emotions can run high during negotiations, leading to irrational decisions or breakdowns in communication. Practice emotional intelligence by remaining calm, composed, and empathetic, even in challenging situations. Manage conflict constructively and focus on problem-solving rather than personal attacks or antagonism.

Practical Tips for Mastering Negotiation Skills:

Practice Active Listening: Listen actively to the other party's concerns, interests, and perspective without interrupting or jumping to conclusions. Pay attention to verbal and nonverbal cues, and paraphrase or summarize their points to demonstrate understanding and build rapport.

Seek Win-Win Solutions: Strive to find win-win solutions that satisfy the interests of both parties and create value beyond what was initially expected. Look for opportunities for trade-offs or compromises that meet everyone's needs while preserving the integrity of the negotiation.

Develop Your BATNA: BATNA, or Best Alternative to a Negotiated Agreement, refers to the course of action you'll take if negotiations fail to reach a satisfactory outcome. Develop and assess your BATNA beforehand to determine your leverage and negotiation power and to avoid settling for unfavorable terms out of desperation.

Use Objective Criteria: Whenever possible, base your negotiation positions on objective criteria, such as market data, industry benchmarks, or independent valuation methods. Using objective criteria strengthens your arguments and increases the likelihood of reaching a fair and equitable agreement.

Practice Role-Playing: Role-playing exercises allow you to simulate negotiation scenarios and practice different strategies, tactics, and communication styles in a low-risk environment. Partner with a colleague, mentor, or coach to role-play various negotiation scenarios and receive feedback on your performance.

Seek Feedback and Learn from Experience: Solicit feedback from peers, mentors, or trusted advisors on your negotiation skills and performance. Reflect on past negotiation experiences, identify areas for improvement, and incorporate lessons learned into your future negotiations to continuously refine and enhance your negotiation skills.

Conclusion:
Mastering negotiation skills is a valuable asset that can open doors to new opportunities, maximize income potential, and achieve favorable outcomes in various aspects of life. By understanding the fundamentals of negotiation, employing

16. Developing a Personalized Investment Strategy Aligned with Your Risk Tolerance and Financial Goals

Creating a personalized investment strategy is a crucial step towards building wealth and achieving your financial aspirations. By aligning your investment approach with your risk tolerance, time horizon, and financial goals, you can maximize returns while managing potential risks effectively. In this article, we'll explore the process of developing a personalized investment strategy tailored to your unique circumstances, preferences, and objectives.

Assessing Your Risk Tolerance:

Before diving into investment decisions, it's essential to assess your risk tolerance—the degree of uncertainty or volatility you're comfortable with regarding your investments. Risk tolerance is influenced by various factors, including your financial situation, investment experience, time horizon, and emotional temperament. Here's how to evaluate your risk tolerance:

Risk Capacity: Assess your financial capacity to withstand potential losses without jeopardizing your financial stability or long-term goals. Consider factors such as your income, expenses, savings, debt levels, and liquidity needs.

Risk Appetite: Evaluate your psychological willingness to accept risk and uncertainty in pursuit of higher returns. Reflect on your emotional reactions to market volatility, past investment experiences, and comfort level with different asset classes.

Risk Perception: Consider your perception of risk and your ability to tolerate fluctuations in the value of your investments. Determine whether you prioritize capital preservation, income generation, or capital appreciation in your investment strategy.

Defining Your Financial Goals:

Once you understand your risk tolerance, clarify your financial goals—both short-term and long-term. Your investment strategy should be aligned with your goals, whether they involve building wealth for retirement, funding education expenses, buying a home, or achieving financial independence. Here's how to define your financial goals effectively:

Identify Specific Objectives: Clearly articulate your financial objectives, including the amount of money you aim to accumulate, the timeframe for achieving your goals, and any milestones along the way.

Prioritize Goals: Rank your financial goals based on their importance, urgency, and feasibility. Focus on goals that are most meaningful to you and have the greatest impact on your financial well-being.

Quantify Goals: Quantify your financial goals in terms of dollar amounts, percentages, or other measurable metrics. Establish realistic targets that are challenging yet attainable given your resources and circumstances.

Consider Trade-Offs: Recognize that achieving certain goals may require trade-offs in terms of risk, return, time horizon, and liquidity. Evaluate the trade-offs involved and adjust your investment strategy accordingly to strike the right balance between risk and reward.

Designing Your Investment Portfolio:

With your risk tolerance and financial goals in mind, design an investment portfolio that reflects your unique preferences and objectives. Your portfolio should be diversified across different asset classes, sectors, and geographic regions to reduce risk and enhance returns. Here's how to construct a well-balanced investment portfolio:

Asset Allocation: Determine the optimal mix of asset classes (e.g., stocks, bonds, cash equivalents, real estate, commodities) based on your risk tolerance, time horizon, and investment objectives. Allocate your assets strategically to achieve diversification and optimize risk-adjusted returns.

Risk Management: Implement risk management techniques, such as asset allocation, diversification, and periodic rebalancing, to mitigate portfolio volatility and preserve capital. Consider incorporating defensive assets, such as bonds or alternative investments, to cushion against market downturns.

Investment Selection: Choose specific investments that align with your investment strategy and meet your criteria for risk, return, liquidity, and tax efficiency. Conduct thorough research, due diligence, and investment analysis to select high-quality assets with favorable growth prospects and income potential.

Monitoring and Review: Regularly monitor the performance of your investment portfolio and review your asset allocation, investment holdings, and overall strategy. Adjust your portfolio as needed to accommodate changes in market conditions, economic outlook, or personal circumstances.

Implementing Your Investment Strategy:

Once you've developed your personalized investment strategy, it's time to put it into action. Implementing your investment strategy involves executing trades, opening investment accounts, and allocating funds according to your asset allocation plan. Here's how to implement your investment strategy effectively:

Select Investment Vehicles: Choose appropriate investment vehicles, such as brokerage accounts, retirement accounts (e.g., 401(k), IRA), mutual funds, exchange-traded funds (ETFs), or individual securities, based on your investment preferences and tax considerations.

Execute Trades: Place buy and sell orders for the investments selected in your asset allocation plan. Pay attention to transaction costs, liquidity, and market timing when executing trades to minimize expenses and optimize execution.

Automate Contributions: Set up automatic contributions or periodic investments to systematically allocate funds to your investment accounts. Automating contributions ensures consistency and discipline in your investment approach, regardless of market fluctuations or external factors.

Reinvest Dividends and Distributions: Reinvest dividends, interest payments, and capital gains distributions to compound your investment returns over time. Reinvesting distributions allows you to benefit from the power of compounding and accelerate the growth of your investment portfolio.

Monitoring and Adjusting Your Strategy:

Finally, regularly monitor the performance of your investment portfolio and make adjustments as needed to stay on track towards your financial goals. Periodically review your asset allocation, investment holdings, and overall strategy to ensure they remain aligned with your risk tolerance and objectives. Rebalance your portfolio periodically to realign your asset allocation with your target allocation and capitalize on investment opportunities as they arise. By staying disciplined, informed, and adaptable, you can navigate changing market conditions and achieve long-term success with your personalized investment strategy.

Conclusion:

Developing a personalized investment strategy aligned with your risk tolerance and financial goals is essential for building wealth, achieving financial independence, and realizing your dreams. By assessing your risk tolerance, defining your financial goals, designing a well-balanced investment portfolio, and implementing your strategy effectively, you can maximize income and investment opportunities while managing risk prudently. Remember to regularly monitor your portfolio, review your investment strategy, and make adjustments as needed to adapt to evolving market conditions and personal circumstances. With diligence, discipline, and a long-term perspective, you can navigate the complexities of investing and create a brighter financial future for yourself and your loved ones.

17. Embracing Continuous Learning and Staying Updated on Financial Trends and Opportunities

In today's rapidly evolving financial landscape, staying informed, adaptable, and proactive is essential for making informed decisions, seizing opportunities, and achieving financial success. Embracing continuous learning allows individuals to expand their knowledge, sharpen their skills, and stay ahead of emerging trends and developments in the financial world. In this article, we'll explore the importance of lifelong learning in finance, practical strategies for staying updated on financial trends and opportunities, and the benefits of adopting a growth mindset in your financial journey.

The Importance of Continuous Learning in Finance:

Continuous learning is the process of acquiring new knowledge, skills, and insights throughout one's life to adapt to changing circumstances, pursue personal growth, and achieve professional excellence. In the realm of finance, ongoing learning is particularly critical due to the dynamic nature of markets, regulations, technologies, and economic conditions. Here's why embracing continuous learning is essential for financial success:

Adaptability: Financial markets are constantly evolving in response to geopolitical events, technological innovations, regulatory changes, and economic trends. Continuous learning enables individuals to adapt to shifting market dynamics, seize new opportunities, and navigate challenges effectively.

Knowledge Acquisition: The field of finance is vast and multifaceted, encompassing areas such as investments, portfolio management, risk management, taxation, estate planning, and financial analysis. Continuous learning allows individuals to deepen their understanding of complex financial concepts, theories, and practices to make informed decisions.

Skill Development: Financial success requires a diverse set of skills, including analytical skills, critical thinking, problem-solving, communication, and decision-making. Continuous learning helps individuals hone these skills and develop competencies that are essential for career advancement and wealth creation.

Risk Mitigation: Staying informed about financial trends, regulations, and best practices enables individuals to identify potential risks and take proactive measures to mitigate them. Continuous learning empowers individuals to make prudent financial decisions and protect their assets from unexpected downturns or disruptions.

Opportunity Recognition: By staying updated on emerging trends, technologies, and investment opportunities, individuals can identify new avenues for growth, diversification, and wealth accumulation. Continuous learning opens doors to innovative strategies, markets, and products that may yield higher returns or lower risk.

Practical Strategies for Staying Updated on Financial Trends and Opportunities:

Read Widely: Stay informed about financial news, trends, and developments by reading reputable sources such as financial publications, industry journals, blogs, and research reports. Subscribe to newsletters, follow financial experts on social media, and join online communities to access timely insights and analysis.

Attend Seminars and Workshops: Participate in seminars, workshops, webinars, and conferences focused on finance, investing, and personal finance topics. These events provide opportunities to learn from industry experts, network with peers, and gain practical knowledge and skills.

Enroll in Courses and Certifications: Take advantage of educational opportunities offered by universities, colleges, and professional organizations to deepen your understanding of finance and acquire relevant certifications or credentials. Online courses, workshops, and certificate programs provide flexible learning options for busy professionals.

Join Professional Associations: Join professional associations and networking groups related to finance, investing, or specific areas of interest (e.g., CFA Institute, Financial Planning Association). Participating in professional communities allows you to exchange ideas, share experiences, and access resources for ongoing learning and development.

Engage with Financial Advisors: Build relationships with trusted financial advisors, planners, or mentors who can provide personalized guidance, insights, and recommendations tailored to your individual goals and circumstances. Regular discussions with a knowledgeable advisor can help you stay on track towards financial success and adapt to changing market conditions.

Utilize Online Resources: Leverage online resources such as financial websites, podcasts, webinars, and forums to access educational content, expert opinions, and interactive tools for financial planning, analysis, and decision-making. Take advantage of free or low-cost resources to expand your knowledge and stay updated on relevant topics.

Adopting a Growth Mindset in Finance:

In addition to acquiring knowledge and skills, adopting a growth mindset is crucial for continuous learning and personal development in finance. A growth mindset is characterized by a belief in one's ability to learn, grow, and improve over time through effort, practice, and resilience. Here's how to cultivate a growth mindset in your financial journey:

Embrace Challenges: View financial challenges, setbacks, and failures as opportunities for learning and growth rather than insurmountable obstacles. Approach new experiences with curiosity, openness, and a willingness to stretch beyond your comfort zone.

Persist in the Face of Adversity: Maintain perseverance and resilience in the pursuit of your financial goals, even in the face of setbacks or obstacles. Learn from failures, adapt your strategies, and keep moving forward with determination and optimism.

Seek Feedback and Reflection: Solicit feedback from peers, mentors, or advisors to gain insights into your strengths, weaknesses, and areas for improvement. Reflect on your experiences, successes, and failures to extract valuable lessons and apply them to future decisions and actions.

Embrace Lifelong Learning: Approach learning as a lifelong journey of growth and discovery, rather than a finite destination. Stay curious, stay hungry for knowledge, and stay open to new ideas, perspectives, and opportunities for learning and development.

Celebrate Progress and Success: Acknowledge and celebrate your progress, achievements, and milestones along the way. Recognize the effort, dedication, and perseverance required to pursue your financial goals and appreciate the value of continuous improvement and self-development.

Conclusion:

Embracing continuous learning and staying updated on financial trends and opportunities is essential for achieving success and fulfillment in your financial journey. By adopting a growth mindset, actively seeking knowledge, and leveraging diverse learning opportunities, you can expand your capabilities, seize new opportunities, and navigate the complexities of the financial landscape with confidence and resilience. Remember that learning is a lifelong process, and each step you take towards personal growth and development brings you closer to realizing your full potential and achieving your financial dreams. Commit to lifelong learning, embrace challenges, and cultivate a mindset of growth and possibility in your pursuit of financial success and well-being.

18. Creating a Legacy Plan to Leave Behind a Lasting Impact on Future Generations

Planning for your legacy involves more than just passing on financial assets; it's about leaving behind a meaningful and enduring impact that transcends generations. Whether it's preserving family values, supporting charitable causes, or passing on wisdom and knowledge, a well-crafted legacy plan ensures that your values, beliefs, and aspirations continue to shape the world long after you're gone. In this article, we'll explore the importance of creating a legacy plan, key elements to consider in your legacy planning process, and practical steps for leaving behind a lasting legacy for future generations.

The Importance of Legacy Planning:

Legacy planning is a proactive process that allows individuals to articulate their values, articulate their values, priorities, and intentions for the future, and ensure that their legacy reflects their personal values, vision, and impact they wish to leave behind. Here are some reasons why legacy planning is essential:

Preserving Family Values: Legacy planning provides an opportunity to pass on cherished family values, traditions, and stories to future generations. By articulating your family's values and principles, you can instill a sense of identity, belonging, and purpose in your descendants.

Supporting Charitable Causes: Legacy planning allows you to support charitable organizations, causes, or initiatives that are meaningful to you and align with your values and beliefs. By incorporating philanthropy into your legacy plan, you can make a positive impact on society and leave behind a legacy of generosity and compassion.

Empowering Future Generations: Legacy planning empowers future generations with resources, opportunities, and guidance to pursue their dreams, aspirations, and passions. By providing financial support, educational scholarships, or mentorship programs, you can equip your descendants with the tools they need to thrive and succeed in life.

Fostering Family Unity: Legacy planning fosters communication, collaboration, and unity among family members by involving them in discussions about shared values, goals, and aspirations. By engaging in open dialogue and decision-making processes, you can strengthen family bonds and build a sense of solidarity across generations.

Key Elements of a Legacy Plan:

A comprehensive legacy plan encompasses various elements that reflect your values, priorities, and aspirations for the future. While each legacy plan is unique to the individual or family, some common elements to consider include:

Estate Planning: Drafting a will, establishing trusts, and designating beneficiaries to ensure the orderly transfer of assets and property to heirs or beneficiaries according to your wishes.

Charitable Giving: Incorporating philanthropy into your legacy plan by supporting charitable organizations, establishing a family foundation, or creating donor-advised funds to address pressing social issues and leave a positive impact on society.

Family Governance: Establishing guidelines, structures, and mechanisms for decision-making, conflict resolution, and wealth stewardship within the family, such as family councils, charters, or constitutions.

Education and Mentorship: Providing educational opportunities, financial support, and mentorship programs for younger generations to foster personal and professional development and pass on knowledge, skills, and values.

Healthcare Directives: Creating advance directives, healthcare proxies, or powers of attorney to ensure that your medical wishes are honored and your healthcare decisions are made according to your preferences in the event of incapacity.

Personal Legacy Statements: Articulating your personal values, beliefs, life lessons, and reflections in a written legacy statement or ethical will to share with future generations and convey the essence of who you are and what you stand for.

Practical Steps for Legacy Planning:

Reflect on Your Values: Take time to reflect on your core values, beliefs, and principles that you want to instill in future generations. Consider the legacy you want to leave behind and the impact you hope to make on your family, community, and society.

Engage Family Members: Involve family members in the legacy planning process by soliciting their input, listening to their perspectives, and incorporating their aspirations into the plan. Foster open communication, mutual respect, and collaboration to ensure that everyone's voice is heard and valued.

Seek Professional Guidance: Consult with estate planners, financial advisors, attorneys, and other professionals with expertise in legacy planning to help you navigate complex legal, financial, and tax considerations and develop a comprehensive legacy plan tailored to your needs and objectives.

Review and Update Regularly: Periodically review and update your legacy plan to reflect changes in your life circumstances, family dynamics, financial situation, and external factors. Stay flexible and adaptable in your approach to legacy planning to ensure that your plan remains relevant and effective over time.

Communicate Your Intentions: Clearly communicate your intentions, wishes, and expectations to your family members, beneficiaries, and trusted advisors to ensure that your legacy plan is understood and implemented according to your wishes. Encourage open dialogue, transparency, and honesty in discussions about your legacy.

Live Your Values: Lead by example and live your values authentically in your daily life, interactions, and decisions. Your actions speak louder than words and serve as a powerful testament to the legacy you wish to leave behind for future generations.

Conclusion:

Legacy planning is a proactive and intentional process that empowers individuals to shape their lasting impact on the world and future generations. By articulating your values, priorities, and aspirations, and developing a comprehensive legacy plan that reflects your personal vision, you can create a legacy that transcends material wealth and leaves a meaningful and enduring impact on the lives of others. Whether it's preserving family values, supporting charitable causes, or empowering future generations, legacy planning allows you to leave behind a legacy that reflects the essence of who you are and the values you hold dear. Start the legacy planning process today and take proactive steps to ensure that your legacy lives on for generations to come.

19. Practicing Mindfulness and Gratitude in Managing Wealth and Abundance

In the pursuit of wealth and abundance, it's easy to get caught up in the relentless pursuit of more—more money, more possessions, more success. However, true wealth and abundance extend beyond material possessions and financial success; they encompass a sense of fulfillment, contentment, and well-being that arises from gratitude and mindfulness. By incorporating mindfulness and gratitude into your approach to managing wealth, you can cultivate a deeper appreciation for the present moment, foster a sense of abundance in your life, and enhance your overall financial well-being. In this article, we'll explore the importance of practicing mindfulness and gratitude in managing wealth and abundance, and provide practical strategies for incorporating these principles into your financial journey.

Understanding Mindfulness and Gratitude:

Mindfulness: Mindfulness is the practice of being fully present and aware of your thoughts, feelings, sensations, and surroundings without judgment. It involves paying attention to the present moment with openness, curiosity, and acceptance, rather than dwelling on the past or worrying about the future. Mindfulness allows you to cultivate a deeper connection to yourself, others, and the world around you, fostering a sense of clarity, peace, and resilience amidst life's challenges.

Gratitude: Gratitude is the practice of recognizing and appreciating the abundance, blessings, and positive aspects of your life, no matter how small or seemingly insignificant. It involves cultivating a mindset of thankfulness, generosity, and appreciation for the people, experiences, and opportunities that enrich your life. Gratitude shifts your focus from what you lack to what you have, fostering feelings of contentment, joy, and fulfillment.

The Importance of Mindfulness and Gratitude in Managing Wealth:

Enhanced Financial Well-Being: Practicing mindfulness and gratitude can improve your overall financial well-being by reducing stress, anxiety, and fear related to money and wealth. By cultivating a sense of inner peace and contentment, you can approach financial decisions with greater clarity, confidence, and intentionality, leading to more positive outcomes and a healthier relationship with money.

Increased Abundance Mindset: Mindfulness and gratitude help shift your mindset from scarcity to abundance, allowing you to recognize and appreciate the abundance that already exists in your life. Instead of focusing solely on what you lack or desire, you can acknowledge and celebrate the abundance of resources, opportunities, and blessings that surround you, fostering a sense of abundance consciousness and empowerment.

Improved Decision-Making: By practicing mindfulness, you can develop greater self-awareness, emotional regulation, and cognitive clarity, which are essential for making sound financial decisions. Mindfulness allows you to observe your thoughts, impulses, and motivations without being driven by them, enabling you to make decisions aligned with your values, goals, and priorities.

Enhanced Relationships: Gratitude cultivates a sense of connection, empathy, and appreciation in your relationships with others, including family, friends, colleagues, and community members. By expressing gratitude for the support, love, and contributions of others, you strengthen interpersonal bonds, build trust, and foster a sense of reciprocity and goodwill, which can positively impact your social and professional networks.

Practical Strategies for Practicing Mindfulness and Gratitude in Managing Wealth:

Daily Gratitude Practice: Start each day by reflecting on three things you're grateful for, whether it's the love of family, the beauty of nature, or the opportunities for growth and learning in your life. Keep a gratitude journal or use a gratitude app to record your daily reflections and reinforce a mindset of appreciation.

Mindful Spending: Practice mindfulness when making purchasing decisions by pausing to consider whether a purchase aligns with your values, needs, and long-term goals. Avoid impulsive or mindless spending by taking a moment to reflect on the true value and utility of the item or experience you're considering.

Savoring Moments of Abundance: Take time to savor moments of abundance and prosperity in your life, whether it's enjoying a delicious meal, spending quality time with loved ones, or achieving a milestone or accomplishment. Cultivate a sense of appreciation for the richness and fullness of each moment, rather than rushing to the next thing.

Gratitude in Adversity: Practice gratitude even in challenging times by focusing on the lessons, growth opportunities, and silver linings that emerge from adversity. Acknowledge the resilience, strength, and support that sustain you during difficult times, and express gratitude for the opportunity to learn and grow from life's experiences.

Generosity and Giving: Cultivate a spirit of generosity by sharing your wealth, resources, and time with others in need. Whether through charitable donations, volunteer work, or acts of kindness, giving back to others not only benefits those in need but also fills your heart with joy and gratitude for the opportunity to make a positive difference in the world.

Conclusion:

Practicing mindfulness and gratitude in managing wealth and abundance is not only beneficial for your financial well-being but also for your overall happiness, fulfillment, and sense of purpose in life. By cultivating mindfulness, you can approach financial decisions with clarity, intentionality, and compassion, leading to greater financial stability and peace of mind. By embracing gratitude, you can cultivate a sense of abundance consciousness, appreciation, and generosity that enriches your relationships, enhances your experiences, and magnifies the blessings in your life. Start incorporating mindfulness and gratitude into your financial journey today and experience the transformative power of living a life of wealth and abundance, both inside and out.

20. Building a Supportive Network of Mentors and Peers for Ongoing Education and Accountability

Creating a supportive network of mentors and peers is essential for personal and professional growth, accountability, and success. Whether you're pursuing financial goals, advancing your career, or striving for personal development, surrounding yourself with a diverse group of mentors and peers can provide invaluable guidance, encouragement, and motivation along the way. In this article, we'll explore the importance of building a supportive network, practical strategies for connecting with mentors and peers, and the benefits of ongoing education and accountability in your journey towards success.

The Importance of a Supportive Network:

Guidance and Mentorship: Mentors provide valuable insights, advice, and guidance based on their knowledge, experience, and expertise. They can offer perspective, wisdom, and practical tips to help you navigate challenges, overcome obstacles, and achieve your goals more efficiently.

Accountability and Motivation: Peers can serve as accountability partners, holding you accountable to your commitments, goals, and deadlines. By sharing your progress, challenges, and achievements with peers, you can stay motivated, focused, and accountable to your aspirations.

Networking and Opportunities: Building relationships with mentors and peers expands your professional network, opening doors to new opportunities, collaborations, and connections. Networking with like-minded individuals allows you to exchange ideas, share resources, and access valuable insights and perspectives from diverse backgrounds and experiences.

Strategies for Connecting with Mentors and Peers:

Identify Your Goals and Needs: Clarify your goals, aspirations, and areas where you could benefit from guidance or support. Determine the specific skills, knowledge, or expertise you're seeking in mentors and the qualities you value in peer relationships.

Research Potential Mentors: Identify individuals who possess the expertise, experience, or qualities you admire and respect. Look for mentors within your industry, profession, or community who have achieved success in areas relevant to your goals and aspirations.

Reach Out and Build Relationships: Initiate contact with potential mentors through networking events, professional associations, social media platforms, or mutual connections. Express genuine interest in their work, achievements, and insights, and seek opportunities to engage in meaningful conversations or interactions.

Be Open to Learning: Approach mentorship as a two-way exchange of knowledge, where both parties can learn from each other's experiences, perspectives, and expertise. Be receptive to feedback, advice, and constructive criticism, and demonstrate a willingness to grow and develop.

Cultivate Peer Relationships: Seek out peers who share your interests, values, and aspirations and are committed to personal and professional growth. Join networking groups, mastermind communities, or online forums where you can connect with like-minded individuals and engage in collaborative learning and support.

Benefits of Ongoing Education and Accountability:

Continuous Learning: Engaging with mentors and peers provides ongoing opportunities for learning, growth, and skill development. By staying curious, open-minded, and receptive to new ideas and perspectives, you can expand your knowledge, expertise, and capabilities over time.

Personal Development: Mentorship and peer support facilitate personal development by fostering self-awareness, self-confidence, and self-improvement. Through constructive feedback, encouragement, and mentorship, you can identify strengths, weaknesses, and areas for growth and take proactive steps to enhance your personal and professional skills.

Goal Achievement: Accountability from mentors and peers helps you stay focused, motivated, and disciplined in pursuit of your goals. Regular check-ins, progress reports, and support from your network provide the structure, encouragement, and accountability needed to overcome obstacles, stay on track, and achieve success.

Networking Opportunities: Building relationships with mentors and peers expands your professional network and opens doors to new opportunities, collaborations, and connections. Networking with individuals who share your interests, values, and aspirations creates synergies, fosters collaboration, and enhances your visibility and reputation within your industry or community.

Conclusion:

Building a supportive network of mentors and peers is essential for ongoing education, accountability, and success in your personal and professional endeavors. By connecting with mentors who can provide guidance, wisdom, and expertise, and cultivating peer relationships based on mutual support, encouragement, and collaboration, you can accelerate your growth, achieve your goals, and realize your full potential. Embrace the power of mentorship and peer support in your journey towards success, and invest in building meaningful relationships that nurture your personal and professional development. Remember that mentorship is not just about receiving guidance; it's also about giving back, sharing your knowledge, and paying it forward to support others on their path to success. Together, with the support of a strong network, you can achieve greater heights and make a meaningful impact in your life and the lives of those around you.

www.ingramcontent.com/pod-product-compliance
Lightning Source LLC
Chambersburg PA
CBHW071056290526
45795CB00004B/1521